Bridgestone
BOOKS

Native American Life

Tepees

by June Preszler

Consultant:
Rebecca West, Curatorial Assistant
Plains Indian Museum
Buffalo Bill Historical Center
Cody, Wyoming

Capstone
press

Mankato, Minnesota

Bridgestone Books are published by Capstone Press,
151 Good Counsel Drive, P.O. Box 669, Mankato, Minnesota 56002.
www.capstonepress.com

Library of Congress Cataloging-in-Publication Data
Preszler, June, 1954–
Tepees / by June Preszler.
    p. cm.—(Bridgestone books. Native American life)
    Includes bibliographical references and index.
    ISBN 0-7368-3727-2 (hardcover)
    1. Tipis. 2. Indians of North America—Dwellings. 3. Tipis—Design and construction. I. Title.
II. Series: Bridgestone Books: Native American life (Mankato, Minn.)
E98.D9P74 2005
690'.8'08997—dc22   2004011426

Summary: A brief introduction to tepees, including the materials, construction, and people who lived in
    these traditional Native American dwellings.

Editorial Credits
Katy Kudela, editor; Jennifer Bergstrom, designer; Kelly Garvin, photo researcher;
    Scott Thoms, photo editor

Photo Credits
Corbis, 14; Corbis/Geoffrey Clements, 8; The Denver Public Library, 12, 16; James P. Rowan, 4;
Kit Breen, cover; Marilyn "Angel" Wynn, 1, 10; Stock Montage Inc./The Newberry Library/Edward
Curtis, 18, 20; Western History Collections, University of Oklahoma Library, 6

1 2 3 4 5 6 10 09 08 07 06 05

Table of Contents

What Is a Tepee?

Tepees are cone-shaped tents. Many Native Americans used them as homes. Tepees were made with tree poles and buffalo **hides**. When buffalo became hard to find, people used **canvas** cloth.

Tepees were made in different sizes. Most tepees were as tall as a one-story building. Native Americans built tepees about 14 feet (4 meters) high and 13 feet (4 meters) around. Some tepees were twice as large.

◀ Tree poles and buffalo hides or canvas formed a cone-shaped tepee.

6

Who Lived in a Tepee?

Some Plains Indian **tribes** lived in tepees. Plains Indian tribes included the Arapaho, Sioux, Pawnee, and many others. They lived on the Great Plains of central North America.

Tepees were good homes for life on the Great Plains. They offered shelter from snow and rain. Tepees were also easy to move.

Today, the Plains Indians live in modern houses. Tribes still build and use tepees for **ceremonies**.

◀ Most tepees were home to a single family.

Gathering Materials

The Plains Indians used tree poles to build the tepee **frame**. They needed about 15 young pine trees. Men cut down the trees and removed the branches and bark.

Buffalo hides covered the tepee frame. It took eight to 15 hides to cover one tepee.

Women gathered dried grass and brush. They used the dried grass and brush in cold weather to fill the tepee **liners**. Tepee liners hung from the inside poles of the tepee. The filled liners helped keep the tepee warm.

◄ Men hunted buffalo and brought the hides to the women. Women used the hides for tepee covers.

Preparing the Materials

Women treated the buffalo hides. They cleaned off the hair and removed the fat. Next they softened the hides. Women soaked the hides in water or rubbed them with buffalo brains, fat, and livers. The hides were then stretched on a rack to dry.

Women used the dried hides to make a tepee cover. They sewed the soft, dry hides together with buffalo **sinew**. They cut a door opening and sewed smoke flaps near the top of the tepee cover.

◄ Women stretched the hides and dried them in the sun.

Building a Tepee

Women carefully built the tepee. They tied three strong poles together to form a **tripod**. They added thinner poles to make a cone-shaped frame. Women wrapped the buffalo skin cover around this frame.

Women made sure the tepee cover stayed in place. Wooden stakes held the cover to the ground. Small sticks called lacing pins closed the door opening. The women also attached poles to the smoke flaps. The poles let them close the flaps during wind or rain.

◀ Women helped each other build their tepees.

Inside a Tepee

Family life inside the tepee was pleasant. People cooked, ate meals, and slept on furs and blankets inside the tepee. They talked, sewed, and welcomed visitors.

Well-built tepees were comfortable. During the day, light shone through the smoke hole and door opening. At night, a fire warmed everyone inside. The smoke rose up through the smoke hole to the outside.

◄ People sat and slept around the inside edges of the tepee.

Tepee Villages

The Plains Indians lived in villages. In each village, many tepees usually formed a circle. All the tepee doors faced east to the rising sun.

The center of the village was special. People held dances and ceremonies there. Important tribal members had their tepees set up close to the center.

Winter villages were set up differently. In cold weather, people camped in areas along rivers.

◄ The center of the village served as a gathering area for the tribe.

Special Tepees

Large tepees had special uses. A council lodge was often set up near the middle of the village. Tribal leaders held meetings in the large council lodge.

Some tepees had special decorations. The Plains Indians sometimes painted their tepees. Painted tepees had animals, stars, and other designs drawn on them.

◀ Some people painted special designs on their tepees.

Moving Tepees

The Plains Indians did not stay in one place. They moved when the seasons changed. Hunters followed the moving animal herds.

When they moved, the Plains Indians took apart their tepees. They carried their tepees and other belongings on a **travois**. Dogs or horses pulled this triangle-shaped frame.

Tepees are still used today. Tribes build tepees for special events. In summer, many people also use tepees for camping.

◄ The Plains Indians used a travois to move from camp to camp.

Glossary

canvas (KAN-vuhss)—a type of strong cloth

ceremony (SER-uh-moh-nee)—formal actions, words, and often music performed to mark an important occasion

frame (FRAYM)—the structure of a tepee

hide (HIDE)—the skin of an animal

liner (LINE-ur)—animal skins or pieces of canvas sewn together to line the bottom half of a tepee

sinew (SIN-yoo)—a strong piece of body tissue that connects muscle to bone

travois (truh-VOY)—the frame used to move belongings

tribe (TRIBE)—a group of people who share the same ancestors, customs, and laws

tripod (TRYE-pod)—a stand with three legs

Read More

Adams, McCrea. *Tipi.* Native American Homes. Vero Beach, Fla.: Rourke, 2001.

Goble, Paul. *Storm Maker's Tipi.* New York: Atheneum Books for Young Readers, 2001.

Internet Sites

FactHound offers a safe, fun way to find Internet sites related to this book. All of the sites on FactHound have been researched by our staff.

Here's how:
1. Visit *www.facthound.com*
2. Type in this special code **0736837272** for age-appropriate sites. Or enter a search word related to this book for a more general search.
3. Click on the **Fetch It** button.

FactHound will fetch the best sites for you!

Index